ROSS RICHIE CEO & Founder • JACK CUMMINS President • MARK SMYLIE Chief Creative Officer • MATT GAGNON Editor-in-Chief • FILIP SABLIK VP of Publishing & Marketing • STEPHEN CHRISTY VP of Development
LANCE KREITER VP of Licensing & Merchandising • PHIL BARBARO VP of Finance • BRYCE CARLSON Managing Editor • MEL CAYLO Marketing Manager • SCOTT NEWMAN Production Design Manager • DAFNA PLEBAN Editor • SHANNON WATTERS Editor
ERIC HARBURN Editor • REBECCA TAYLOR Editor • CHRIS ROSA Assistant Editor • ALEX GALER Assistant Editor • WHITNEY LEOPARD Assistant Editor • JASMINE AMIRI Assistant Editor • MIKE LOPEZ Production Designer
HANNAH NANCE PARTLOW Production Designer • DEVIN FUNCHES E-Commerce & Inventory Coordinator • BRIANNA HART Executive Assistant • AARON FERRARA Operations Assistant • JOSÉ MEZA Sales Assistant

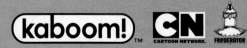

ADVENTURE TIME WITH FIONNA AND CAKE Scholastic Edition, December 2013. Published by KaBOOM!, a division of Boom Entertainment, Inc. ADVENTURE TIME,
CARTOON NETWORK, the logos, and all related characters and elements are trademarks of and © Cartoon Network. (S13) All rights reserved. Originally published in single
magazine form as ADVENTURE TIME WITH FIONNA AND CAKE 1-6. © Cartoon Network. (S13) All rights reserved. KaBOOM!™ and the KaBOOM! logo are trademarks
of Boom Entertainment, Inc., registered in various countries and categories. All characters, events, and institutions depicted herein are fictional. Any similarity between
any of the names, characters, persons, events, and/or institutions in this publication to actual names, characters, and persons, whether living or dead, events, and/or
institutions is unintended and purely coincidental. KaBOOM! does not read or accept unsolicited submissions of ideas, stories, or artwork.

For information regarding the CPSIA on this printed material, call: (203) 595-3636 and provide reference RICH# - 524055. A catalog record of this book
is available from OCLC and from the KaBOOM! website, www.kaboom-studios.com, on the Librarians Page.

BOOM! Studios, 5670 Wilshire Boulevard, Suite 450, Los Angeles, CA 90036-5679. Printed in USA. First Printing.
ISBN: 976-1-60886-407-2. eISBN: 978-1-61398-261-7

"ADVENTURE TIME" CREATED BY

Pendleton Ward

WRITTEN AND ILLUSTRATED BY

Natasha Allegri

Colors by Natasha Allegri & Patrick Seery

with Betty Liang (Chapter 6)

LETTERS BY
Britt Wilson

COVER BY
Natasha Allegri
Colors by Amanda Thomas

ASSISTANT EDITOR   EDITOR
Whitney Leopard   Shannon Watters

TRADE DESIGN BY
Stephanie Gonzaga
with Hannah Nance Partlow

With Special Thanks to Marisa Marionakis, Rick Blanco, Curtis Lelash,
Laurie Halal-Ono, Keith Mack, Kelly Crews and the
wonderful folks at Cartoon Network.

A long time ago...

...before most things existed...

...there was a woman made out of Fire.

She lived alone...

...in a desert covered
in sand and boulders...

One day, she discovered...

...if she kissed a boulder...

...her flames would melt it, turning it into a little happy molten baby.

And she was no longer **alone**.

For a long time, she loved and protected all of them like a mother...

...until the first time it ever

RAINED.

Each raindrop
that hit her
weakened
and shrank her...

...until her
molten babies
towered over
her...

...and realized
it was their turn
to protect her.

They gathered
around her,
shielding her from the rain...

...but it transformed them
back into their original
boulder form.

And even though she's safe,
she's trapped,
and her lava tears fill up her home
and flow out into the sea...

...creating places for new life to live on.

And THAT'S my story about where volcanoes come from!

Cake, your bedtime stories are awful.

Hmmm...

There was no gut-kicking or butt-punching or—

GAAASP!

Fionna...

...stories don't need action to be good!

They just gotta make you feel somethin' in your heart-pit.

Well... your story just made me depressed.

Oh...

I'm sorry.

AAAH! Baby fire lions!
Why are they out in the rain? It's hurting them!
It looks like they're running from something...

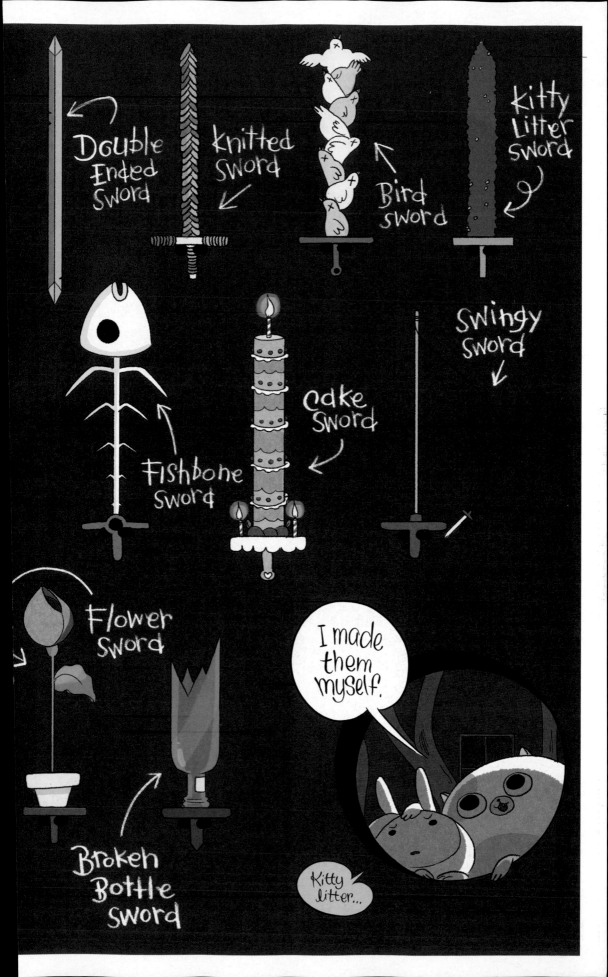

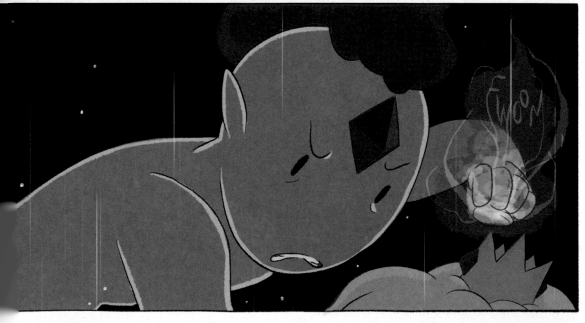

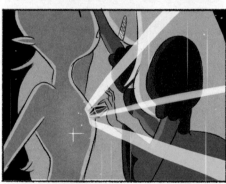

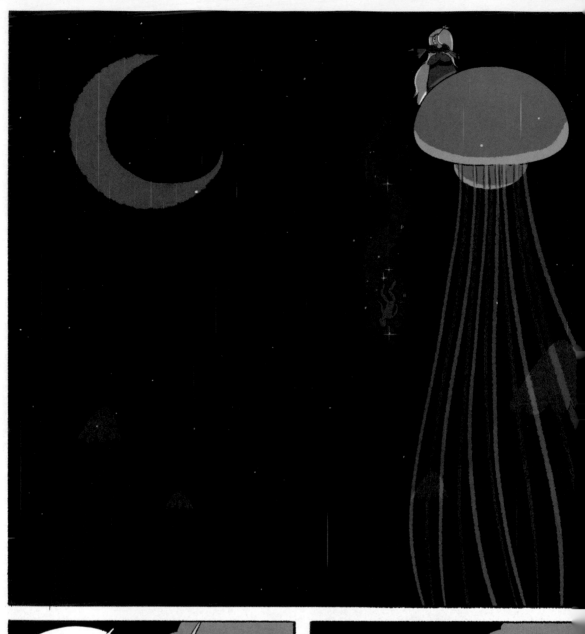

Ice Queen, you better get OUTTA HERE, LADY!
whoa...
And Fionna, you better not be checkin' that guy out!
AHHH!!!!

Ahh, the rain is stopping...
Let those hot little babies go, Ice Queen!
GRRR!

CAKE, I DON'T TAKE ORDERS FROM ANIMALS THAT HACK UP HAIRBALLS.

GAAAASP!

reeeak

THUMP

SLAM

No one talks to Cake like that!

SHING!

OOF!

ACK!

thud

thud

PLEH.

WHA....?

ONE LITTLE HIT AND YOUR SWORD BREAKS? WHAT A POOPY SWORD!

It's kitty-litter. Of **course** it's poopy!

It's SUPER POOPY.

Will you check on your friend in my attic?

Something doesn't feel right...

CREEAK

Ah....?!

AHHHHH!!!

WHAT?! WHAT IS IT?!

We gotta get back to the tree-house!

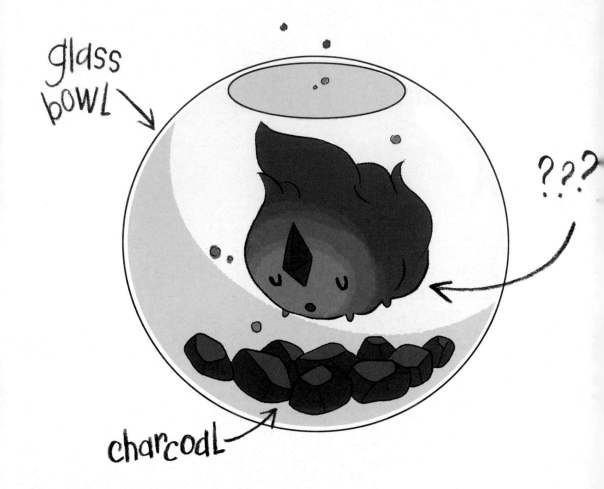

glass bowl

???

charcodl

what happened to him?

He says he needs
to find his Lion Pride so he
can protect his family's
babies from the rain
and the Ice Queen 'til
monsoon season is over...

He also says he's hungry.

Oh, I might have something in my backpack!

A match!

Do fire boogers eat matches

Myam

gloomp

Fwoosh!

Ha ha!

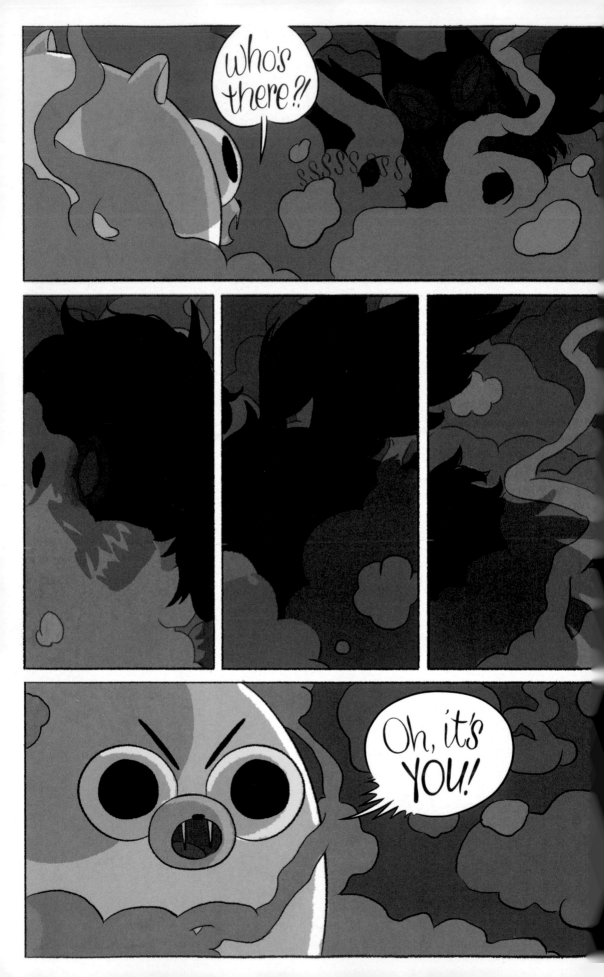

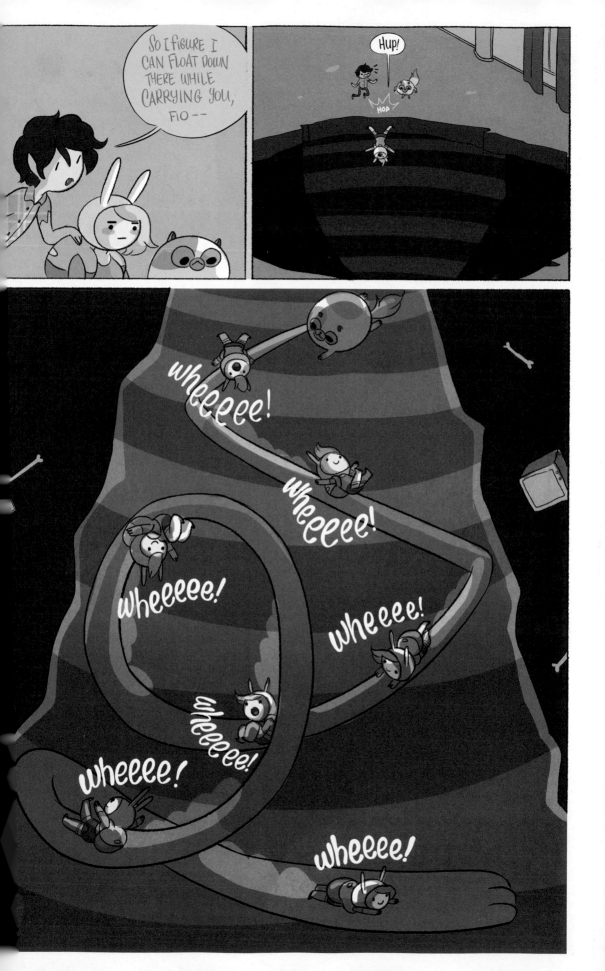

THIS WAY...

Oh, it's cuter than I thought it would be in here.

O...KAY

kukukuku

GAUWAH

CHOMP

fshhh

OW DOES MY FIST TASTE?!

POOM.

...

AAAAAAHHH!!!

...

Fionna...?

You're awake!

Fionna, you saved me...

Why didn't you guys invite me to boy's night?

...

...

You guys usually always invite me!

If I was here I wou have been ab to save you rig away! I just wan protect you gu from puddin and cand skulls and—

EEEEEH...

ALRIGHT GUMBALL, LET'S NOT HIDE IT FROM HER ANYMORE.

IT'S JUST MAKIN' HER SAD.

Okay, okay, you right

MEOW MEOW!

Oh!

You're awake!

GASP!!

MEOW

You're made of fire?

You're perfect!

You go in my oven!

HEY!

You can't just go stickin' him anywhere! He's a person with feelings, not a thing you get to cram into a bake box!

I think he's ok with it.

PURR PURR PURR

STEP 1

STEP 2

click

STEP 3

STEP 4

FWOOSH!

To be on the
cusp of

IMPOSSIBLE
BEAUTY

has been my curse
since the day I was born...

Today, my quest for ultimate beauty will come to an end...
shaaaaaaaaaaaaaaaaaa
aaaaaaaaahh
VYOOM
Gleam

AND SOON...

#1 Hot Guy

I've never been so...

...fulfilled and happy...

Uh?

Uhhhhgh...

I'm...alive?

I'm trapped...

TAP
TAP

eh?

FIONNA.

GIVE ME BACK MY WAND-SWORD-THINGY!

How do you know I even took it?

...cause you always snack when you steal...

FULL OF BEANS

...you weirdo.

HEY! SHE'S STEALIN' OUR BEAUTIFUL PRINCE!

GET HER!

GET THE PRINCE!

Save me, Fionna!

CAPTURE THE PRINCE!

Wait! Stop!

I know you think Lumpy Space Prince is good lookin' now, but don. Let him manipulate your maiden heart. with his weird handsomenes

I know that a beautiful man can turn any lady into a beast...

... but I also know, deep down inside, you're all kir Caring, thoughtful creature

MOW.

Wuh...

WOW!

Cake, did you make him this funny outfit?

Yeah, you like it?

Yeah, I like it!

Cake, I can't fight in this stupid outfit!

We don't need to fight, we just gotta trick her!

And my costume are so awesome she's not gonna even know wha happened!

Wenk.

...

...

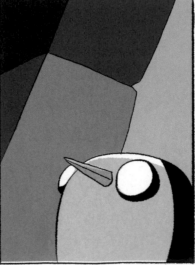

weh—

EXCUSE MY SERVANT'S HORRIBLE MANNERS!

I'M SO GLAD YOU COULD MAKE IT, FLAME PRINCE.

I'M SO SORRY ABOUT OUR HORRIBLE MISUNDERSTANDING EARLIER TODAY.

IF I HAD KNOWN YOU WERE ROYALTY, LIKE MYSELF, I WOULD HAVE DEFINITELY **NOT** BEATEN UP YOUR LITTLE BUDDIES.

BUT I'M GLAD YOU AGREED TO MEET UP WITH ME FOR A—

TURN...

...

I GUESS IT'S A DOUBLE DATE WITH ONE OF YOUR UGLIER FIRE LIONS.

COME ON IN, I'VE PREPARED A DINNER BY CANDLELIGHT.

*poo
**HAW HAW!!

A cat that didn't hate water...

...Saved from drowning by a river nymph.

And when the cat found out the very mortal river nymph was in love with an immortal...

...she said,

"As a cat, I've lived five lives now, and I've seen and heard of a lost treasure that can help you live forever, too."

But the river nymph declined,

"My mortality is what makes all of this so precious to me."

But the cat, so intent on repaying the river nymph back for saving its life, didn't listen, and left for the cave to find the treasure.

The cat managed to escape most of the dangers within the cave until...

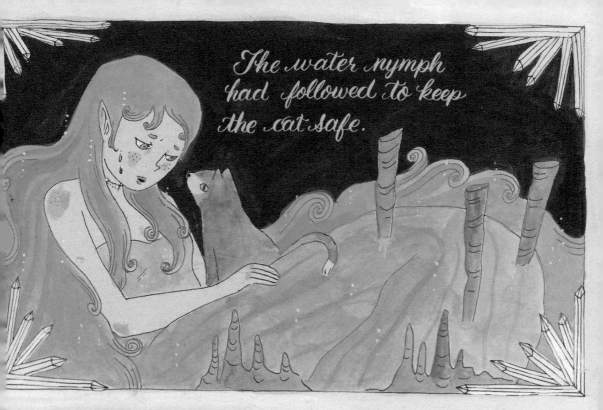

The water nymph had followed to keep the cat safe.

Realizing how injured she was, the cat cried,

"You've saved me twice now, please let me help you!"

When the cat didn't get a response...

...the cat
repaid its debt.

GNAW

Ah?

Hm?

chomp chomp

She did it...?

She took the salt crystal out before midnight ...

THOUGHT WHAT I
[N]EEDED WAS THE LOVE
[O]F A
[PR]INCE...

... UNTIL I FOUND THESE FLAME ELEMENTALS.

BUT THIS CRYSTAL MANAGED TO HARNESS

EVEN MORE WARMTH THAN THE BOTH OF THOSE COMBINED.

GLEAM

VUUURR

what is she--?

TSSS...

Vyoom

Ping

THERE'S SO MUCH STRANGE MAGIC IN THIS WORLD...

SPLish

Tsss..

TSSS..

...BE CAREFUL WITH IT, FIONNA.

WOOSH

ROAR

AHH, EVERYTHING'S MELTING!

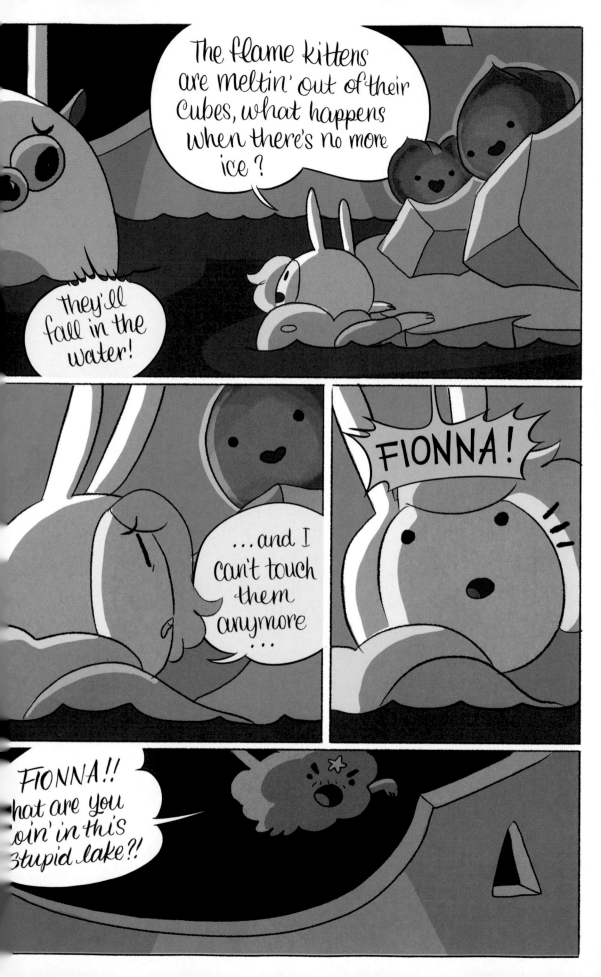

Listen, I tried bein' nice, but I'm still not like, **PHYSICALLY** hot, so I want that wand back.

Sorry Fionna, after he forced me to tell him where you were, he dragged me along.

LSP, I don't have time for this, I--

GGGRRAWWW

CRK!

AH, IT'S TRYING TO MAKE OUT WITH ME!!

CHOMP!

Cover Gallery

Issue #1A
Jen Bennett
Colors by Lisa Moore

Issue #2A
Chad Thomas
Colors by Zack Sterling

Issue #3A
Natasha Allegri
Colors by Amanda Thomas

Issue #4A
Natasha Allegri

Issue #5A
Natasha Allegri
Colors by Amanda Thomas

Issue #6A
Natasha Allegri